BODY LANGUAGE FOR RADICAL RELATIONSHIPS

DISCOVER AND MASTER HOW TO READ BODY LANGUAGE TO YOUR ADVANTAGE!

DR. MARCUS S. BENSON

ISBN-13:978-1502595447

ISBN-10: 1502595443

Published by:

MB Relationship Coaching & Consultancy, Ireland.

23 Earls Court,

Athy,

Co. Kildare.

Ireland.

DEDICATION

This book is dedicated to Sophie and Toju Anwani-Gold.

CONTENTS

ACKNOWLEDGMENTS.

My special thanks goes to the almighty God, the author and the finisher of our faith for his inspiration through the Holy spirit to put this book together.

I value the input and contributions of the members of staff of MB Relationship Coaching & Consultancy to making this book a reality.

Thanks to all those who helped me with typesetting and editing of the final manuscript when my own work schedule became so pressing.

CHAPTER ONE

COMPREHENSION OF BODY LANGUAGE WITH FACILITY

The comprehension of body language will save you loads of problems and heartaches in your relationships. Moreover, it can also give you the added advantage to capitalize on the moment to take whatever belongs to you. You will no longer be kept in the dark as to what is in the hearts of people. As a master in a chess game, you will be able to predict the next move, of people and quickly plan your strategies to checkmate and win them or beat them to it. Release yourself from being at the receiving end of pains, disappointments, shame and regrets in your relationship with people. When you master the act of understanding body language, you will be like a master chess player who can not be taken by surprise, because you have mastered how to checkmate the other player and win effortlessly.

The best way to comprehend people around you is to know how to interpret their body language. This type of capacity is available for each of us. Body language is expressed by non-verbal communication and the so-called body signs.

It is very easy to comprehend what people say, but the most interesting thing is to get to the things they really mean or do not say in words at all. Every one of us uses non-verbal communication in order to express things. Words and sounds are replaced by gestures and body actions. Body language is considered to be a paralanguage or a part of meta-communication. In a few words, to comprehend body-language is to know what the meaning of everybody's sign is. It is an easy assignment.

Body language has also proved to be extremely useful for legal cases, determining if a witness or a suspect is telling the truth. Normally, officers are being prepared in order to comprehend body language. People can also be evaluated in other domains too. There are many fields of activity where people who apply get validated depending on what their body language expresses.

Another essential field of activity is education. None of the primary level children know how to express how well they feel. It is necessary, thus, for educators to know how children feel through their body language.

There are situations when you have to tell people what to do or express a message without using words. Body language is fundamental in that kind of situation. It can also be merged with verbal communication and it has been proved to be a very efficient method to transmit things if combined in the right way.

CHAPTER TWO

PAY ATTENTION WHEN READING BODY LANGUAGE

The main way to identify how a person really feels is by reading his/her body language. It is very useful for you to understand whether or not the one in front of you is honest and trustworthy, independent of what his/her words sound like.

Nowadays people have learnt how to hide their true feelings and opinions and especially how to hide the truth in many situations. That's another advantage that one can have if achieving the ability to read body language.

People's linguistic abilities are very well developed. The words they say can even have an opposite meaning, or a hidden intention that could never come into light without their body language. If you pay attention to not only people's words, but also how these words are said, you may find out unbelievable, untold things. Close observation is the key word to succeed in this.

The first important things to be observed when learning to read body language are facial expression and tone of the voice. People may have become very good at telling lies, but they can hardly hide their faces or modify their tones. Usually humans try to hide under a different facial expression, hiding the truth in their words and their feelings, so there's a forced image that can be easily identified if you are a good, close observer.

Reading body language to identify if a person is lying is far more efficient than all of those modern devices that have been invented. A machine can always fail when it comes to human emotions, but body language doesn't because people were born with it.

The ability of reading body language can only be developed by another person; it is not a task that a machine could complete. It's a very helpful instrument that anyone can use in many situations. When studying body language you have to concentrate a lot on the eyes and the chin. When someone lies, it's usually hard to look directly in the other's eyes. The cheeks may become inactive while jaw and chin may drop when lying.

If you assimilate well enough the ability of reading body language you could easily get hired and have highly important jobs. Another option, in case you don't want a profession on that, would be to use the right tools and simply ease your life by making a better selection of the people around you, this way transforming for good all your relationships.

NON VERBAL COMMUNICATION

Half of the time people use body language instead of verbal expression to communicate. Sometimes, non-verbal communication is not considered important, but in fact it is the only valuable mean to comprehend what people actually think. There is a certain level of complexity in human behavior, and it becomes hard to understand how people really wish to communicate. There is a certain continuity in the experience of learning about non-verbal communication and the subject is also very attractive. Some gestures can show certain feelings about situations or decisions that people cannot say because of social reasons.

The key is to know how to manage your emotions in case of non-verbal communication. You need to hold your emotions in all unexpected situations such as the announcement of the replacement of your favorite immediate boss from the CEO of the company you work at. In that specific case, you may say something that expresses excitement, but you need to pay attention to your non-verbal language as well, because it can surely lead to some opposite opinion about the new settlement. Normally this kind of situation always happen at work.

Practicing is necessary if you want to master your emotions. You don't have to let things happen randomly and remain quiescent, because it is not an attitude that favors you in your non-verbal communication improvement. First of all you need to make a change in the manner you used to see things. You have to think in a pragmatic manner, detaching yourself emotionally from every person, event or any situation that could possibly happen in the external world. That would be part of the answer.

But there is also an excellent thing regarding non-verbal communication. It means it is a gathering of elements that describe how people around feel and what their reaction would be in front of different situations. This is an essential tool in the process of human comprehension. It can even be considered a form of art and be studied, per se, in order to obtain efficient results from it. You can sometimes be mistaken about certain bodily signs if you don't master well this type of particular knowledge. You have to interact a lot with many people and associate them during this learning experience in order to facilitate the access to their behavior, reactions and reasons.

CHAPTER THREE

SUBSTANTIAL ISSUES RELATED TO MEN'S BODY LANGUAGE

Body language nowadays seems rather unimportant for people, because of the many ways of communication that were invented. Mobile phones, for instance, are now easily replacing gestures and body signs that some years ago could have been used as essential ways to understand people when seeing them face-to-face. But it is still possible to do this in modern times too, by using video calling. Body language's importance should be known by anyone if they pretend to communicate the right message while working or talking to friends.

Men's different states of mind can easily be identified by their facial expressions and moves of their arms and legs. Their body language can show either an aggressive character or a stressed one.

There is a lot of information both online and in print form, such as videos, articles, and books describing men's certain essential aspects of body language. It is very easy to identify a deceptive, too romantic or even threatening type of man if you simply watch a video, read an article or more if you are really interested), or even read a book on this.

An important condition to understand a man's body language is to stay close to him, meaning that he is in confidence with you. However, you need to establish the limit of an acceptable distance between you two, depending on how well you know him; it may also happen to get too close to one another. Always pay attention to his eyes and to direct eye contact—if he hides something he will try to avoid looking straight into yours—and always look somewhere else. The way he holds his head and his feet are also very significant.

Another aspect when referring to men's body language is his culture, such as western or eastern. In different cultures there are different significations about men's body language; the common aspects for the easterners may prove to be offensive or strange for the esterners, or vice versa. If you wish to make or study, it is important to get some basic information on some aspects of that person's culture so that you are not misunderstood in your conversation.

CHAPTER FOUR

DEEP INSIGHT INTO BODY LANGUAGE

It is obvious to say that being able to determine what men are feeling or thinking is in general harder than in women. When it comes to discussing their feelings, men find it to be an agonizing topic, which is why understanding the male body language helps women determine their thoughts, feelings and physical act when they are perhaps flirting. The male body language expresses their feelings so it is helpful for women to learn of these expressions.

Understanding male body language signals such as paying close attention to their eyes, can help a woman determine if they are attracted to her or not. If a man makes direct eye contact and holds his gaze, it is a definite sign of interest. Sometimes a male can feel intimidated by a woman, which is when they avoid eye contact completely or try to avoid it as much as possible. When a man looks at a woman in a triangular manner, such as looking into one of their eyes, then shifting their gaze to the other eye and then finally moving their gaze downwards towards the mouth or the nose, is a clear sign of interest at the woman's appearance. Their pupils enlarge and blink more frequently when expressing physical interest.

The male body language tends to be more dominant because their gestures are normally supposed to say "I'm the boss!" By paying attention to their stance, a woman would be able to judge if they are approachable or not. A man would show dominance by the way he spreads his legs while he sits and observes the situation by reclining back when they are listening. A man who stands up straight pushing his chest out with his hands by his side is definitely displaying confidence and control to be approached by a woman. Very rarely do men show their emotions, unlike women; as a result, if they display any facial expressions it should be considered genuine and taken into consideration by a woman.

When a guy's body is pointing in the direction of a woman it is to display a sign of attraction. The male body language displays its signals in the direction of the woman he is trying to attract. So for those women who are sometimes confused, when a guy faces a woman more, it is a sign of flirting.

Some women find it hard to determine the male body language, but this might be because women look for the most obvious signals or visuals, instead try to determine the variation in their behaviour that can easily give them away. Instead of preying on men to discuss their feelings, women can easily judge the male body language for signs.

CHAPTER FIVE

DEEP INSIGHT INTO FEMALE BODY LANGUAGE

Almost every subject today puts into discussion body language: sports, education, cultural events, public speaking, celebrations, etc. But ooh! We forgot! Did we miss 'female body language'? Let's talk about it as it's a very common subject.

It may seem the most difficult on earth to be interpreted, but still a way to identify how a woman feels compared to another. For men, this is surely an interesting thing: to be able to date a worthy woman and notice what she thinks and how she really reacts to your way of behaving.

First of all it is essential to learn the basics about female body language, because otherwise you can easily get humiliated by being ignored at the moment you try to flirt and read a woman's mind. There are very many methods of learning on this subject. There are online support websites that can help you with it, furnishing a lot of precious information about female body language.

Usually girls never make the first step towards a man, even if they are interested in him. It could be a matter of female pride or simple timidity. But there are cases where you can easily notice that a woman likes you, as she lets you know this directly or by a seductive smile. Notice if a woman feels comfortable with you, if she allows you to touch her, or if she herself touches you on your shoulder while talking. These are clear steps that show her being approachable and available for the next step.

If she keeps adjusting her dress or her hair or simply keeps playing with it, it's a natural internal sign that she is trying to look good in front of you. A woman always tries to look good in front of someone she is attracted to, of someone she likes.

This is not about quantity, but about quality; even the smallest gesture of a woman can be so incredibly attractive for a man. He always has to pay attention during parties or any public gathering on female body language signals to be sure of not missing out meeting the perfect match.

CHAPTER SIX

HOW TO ACTUALLY FLIRT USING BODY LANGUAGE

When talking about corporate scenarios, various body language signs need to be accurately interpreted, as a wrong judgment would really bring serious problems. Body language in flirting area asks for plenty of your attention. One of the most undesirable issues that a wrong interpretation could lead to is sexual harassment. Pitfalls are consequences that really shouldn't happen; this is why interpreting must be done correctly. There are some ways to anticipate such clues.

The "twinkle in the eye" or "biting of the lip" could be in a hypothetical situation interpreted as flirting signs, sent from your boss or one of your work colleagues for instance. But are you sure about it? Pay attention to what you presume because it may also be the wrong interpretation. But if it is true, how are you possibly going to transmit that you are not interested? You will definitely need to decide that. You could also be facing an apparently mistaken touch of the hands. it could also be a signal.

Clues regarding flirting in body language are unlimited and various. When talking about an executive in a company for instance, he will surely use professionalism to solve a matter of this kind, with the purpose of saying, "I'm not interested". One of the methods would be clear out that you are only concerned with the work. There is a very strict stance when talking about personal affairs in the working place in modern times.

This is why one should master well the interpretation of body language signals, especially the flirting area. Clues have to be relevant also. An important thing one has to acquire on flirting body language is experience. The more you stay tuned with people's interaction and socialize with them, the better you'll do with possible flirting situations. You have to easily manage with people real intensions through their body language signs that they transmit. Living and learning is the only way to assimilate in order to become a master in this form of art.

CHAPTER SEVEN

HOW TO COMMUNICATE THROUGH BODY LANGUAGE

Since the beginning of mankind, communication has been developed in many forms. Verbal and non-verbal communication are the two basics used. Verbal communication is known as a direct and clear form of expressing, while a non-verbal one needs to be studied and interpreted through body language and its signals.

Genuine signs are included in body language such as smiles, waves or nods, which are all part of human interactions, as a reaction to our everyday thoughts and feelings that need more than words. Body language is often used to express a lot more than words as being much more complex. Its results also can prove to be more efficient and powerful than words can transmit.

The thumbs up sign, for example, clearly means "good job!" but a fist is always describing fury. If one crosses his arms around his chest as if embracing himself, it means he's creating an unconscious barrier between him and the others.

Psychology studies have been developed to study the relationship between facial gestures and verbal communication. One example is Professor Emeritus of Psychology at the UCLA Albert Mehrabian whose studies and researches were based on the ability to comprehend body language. The results were the following: face to face communication is divided into many smaller or larger parts. Thus, 7% of communication is expressed in verbal words, 38% identified in voice tone and 55% through body language signals. A so-called 7%-38%-55%

rule belongs to familiar situation between two people that can assure that is all going according to normality. But there is always a hidden aspect between the normality rule and body language's code. Body language can transmit a lot more information than the established rules can. Mehrabian's rule only applies in instances where there is direct, face-to-face communication, as there is an ordinary, yet mistaken belief that Mehrabian's 7%-38%-55% rule applies in all situations of communication. It cannot be relevant in the case of e-mail thus no verbal, expressing, no voice tone or any body language signal.

There are some given examples of such signals of body language:

- Looking away: a person's lack of interest;

- Hands on knees: enthusiasm, anxiousness;

- Scratching the chin: doubt;

- Looking down: a person is timid, fearful, compliant, or feels blameworthy.

Think of any other significance they could possibly have.

CHAPTER EIGHT

MORE STUDY ON BODY LANGUAGE

Communication through body language proved to have a lot of influence in our everyday actions, but in a shared manner. If a person expresses confidence and interest through body language, there are many more success opportunities to be taken. Normally our face does not express what we think. Body expressions have a great impact on people's opinions about you, and you have to be cautious so that you can send the right message.

Thoughts and feelings can be easily expressed through body language. Regardless of willing or unwilling body language, behaviors have the power to strengthen or weaken our personality. Both consciously and unconsciously reciprocity can be created by our reading of body language and others reading our body language.

The opinion about a person at a subconscious level means the way we appreciate that person. The reading of body language produces opinions about other people. If some of the gestures of body language of a person that we search for because we don't really know him/her creates for us a concern, the result is not to trust that person. Body language becomes genuine if we use intentional gestures as a method of communication with other people. Forced gestures made up with evident effort and superficiality usually produce unfavorable effects on others. A positive effect instead, can be produced by a confident and relaxed body language behaviour. The key is being positive to yourself so that others can do the same with you.

Holding your head up and keeping straight shoulders always illustrate a positive character, expressing trustworthiness in body language. In a conversation the basic relevant sign of confidence is maintaining a direct eye contact with the person you talk to. Palms of your hands should be opened, arms relaxed at your sides when walking or seated so you can create the right trustable image.

You shouldn't have at all an indifferent or defensive behavior towards a person that you see for the first time. Adopt that position which makes you feel comfortable and relaxed as an assurance. Taking more space around you will give a bigger and more important aspect of your person if that is what you intend to illustrate about yourself.

An honest, warm smile and a handshake are good elements you can use in order to give confidence to the others. But make sure you don't shake hands too hard. These are signs of honesty and trust. Pay attention on the way you breath, because that also tells something about yourself; breathing should be slow and deep in order to show a calm and wise type of character.

CHAPTER NINE

BODY LANGUAGE GESTURES

There is for sure a difference between what people say and think; and this is how body language and reading its signs can help you discover the truth in a person's thinking. Non-verbal communication expressed through body language is an unconscious form of action between people, illustrated in body postures, gestures, eye movements, head movements and others. Recent studies discovered that nearly 60 to 70% of the information transmitted between people is made through body language gestures. Body language can very well indicate the mental outlook or the mood of a person in one particular moment.

Comprehension of body language, gestures is a very large subject to be discussed and its purpose is surely different than just a mean of communication. The main way to comprehend body language is to follow the moves of the head, eyes, upper and lower bodies. There are also the open and closed signals depending on the interest that a person has, or on how timid he is, if he creates a barrier between you two, or if, on the contrary, he shows himself available and confident with you. If barriers are created, by comprehending and mastering good body language, there are some ways to break through it by responding in the right way.

The head gestures illustrated in body language are pretty easy to be interpreted by people; an inclined head clearly means an interest in someone or something they are told of, or shown to. Usually the lack of interest that can be noticed in a lecture hall or in a classroom is illustrated through body language with nodding a lot of the head just to be polite to the one who's reading or speaking in front. In order to think about something, or to make an evaluation, we usually place our hands on our cheek. Touching our nose or scratching it shows lack of trust and refusal of something or someone.

Eyes' behaviour is the most simple body language signal to be interpreted. As it is well known, avoiding to look in someone's eyes means timidity, or even hidden things, as long as looking straight into somebody's eyes means the opposite: confidence or self-trust. Looking up and then to the right means a person is trying to remember something while looking up and then left illustrates creativity and imagination.

The position of the body, the upper and lower parts, can say a lot about a person's character. Disapproval about something that has been told and creating a barrier between him and all the rest of the world is expressed in body language signals by crossing the arms on the chest. If you are feeling relaxed and serene, you usually put your hands behind your back. An erect posture generally expresses self-trust.

CHAPTER TEN

WHAT DOES BODY LANGUAGE MEAN?

Body language consists of body signals and movements of its different parts. Its significance is about what all those gestures tell about the person who makes it, and in what way it could be interpreted.

An erect kind of walking is surely a signal of self-trust, on a recent study version of body language. Standing with your hands on your hips generally may illustrate availability or aggression. The hunching of shoulders and his keeping of his hands in his pockets while walking, the body language signal given corresponds to a feeling of depression.

The position in which a person is seated with his legs crossed and his foot up moving or slightly kicking, is a signal of boredom in body language. Another position is that in which a person is seated with his legs apart; this in body language signals means availability and a relaxed state of mind. Another meaning of boredom can be identified when a person holds his head in his hand or when he continuously inclines his head.

A hand, put on the cheek signifies that a person makes an evaluation or he thinks of something or someone. A person who keeps touching his nose or even rubbing it generally expresses refusal, lack of trust or even hiding something from others. Rubbing the eyes has a similar signification of doubt and lack of trust. If a person keeps his eyes closed and pinches the bridge of his nose, he might probably think of something not very pleasant and also that he is being quite thoughtful.

Open palms normally illustrate correctness and availability of a person in body language signs. Clasping his hands behind his/her back may describe a defensive, furious or even frustrated kind of person. When someone rubs his hands it is a sign of anticipation or eagerness described in body language. If one is seated, holding his hands clasped behind his head and his legs are crossed, this kind of body language paints a picture of a superior kind of person, a person with a great feeling of confidence or even an arrogant type of guy.

There are two possible ways of behaving in body language using fingers: tapping fingers and stealing fingers. When you see a person tapping his fingers, then you have to finish up what you were saying because he has no more patience to listen to you. A person who steals his fingers in body language signals illustrates an authority, a type of feeling that a person has.

A constant touching of the hair or playing with it while having a conversation, in body language has many significations: lack of self-trust, fear, insecurity, agitation, a nervous state of someone. If a person is biting his nails, there are similar meanings in body language as for the touching of the hair.

All of these body language, gestures are part of our daily lives; any time we could meet any kind of such persons with such types of personality. No matter where you find yourself, at work, at home, out with friends, these are very common situations you can face too. Body language signals should be observed in a discreet manner so that the person you observe doesn't realize he's being looked at.

CHAPTER ELEVEN

BODY LANGUAGE SECRETS

Body language is a great form of conversation that is oftentimes not taken into consideration. To uncover its mysteries you must understand perfectly what the person in front of you is trying to illustrate.

Body language secrets are numerous. Recognizing them is just the first step of comprehending this type of communication. A person should also consider the situation in which it is utilized. There are many body language secrets utilized during a conversation. One of them is arm crossing. Depending on the context, this can have different meanings. If it's an intense discussion, the person who crosses arms can suggest that he doesn't agree with what the person in front of him describes. Arms crossing is used in other situations too, for instance, when the weather is bad and someone feels cold. That is why it's critical to acknowledge the context which lie in these body language secrets.

Another key body language sign that everyone should comprehend is eye contact. Messages sent through eye contact are the most valuable signs of a discussion, because if eye contact is not interrupted that indicates confidence. Alternatively, if eye contact is interrupted, that shows shyness and self-esteem absence. In general, eye contact with the other person shows that the two sides agree on what they talk about. People that show interest in what the speaker talks about will be more attentive. If there is less eye contact or no eye contact, that means there is less interest. Some people use eye contact to express their opinions or state of mind. Raising an eyebrow often shows disagreement, while continuous yawning and eye blinking indicates absolute agreement.

Examining other parts of the body like hands, posture or facial expressions will give you the opportunity to comprehend the significance of the discussion better. If the speaker makes constant hand movements that shows interest about the subject, while intermittent fidgeting has the meaning of nervousness. People who shrug their shoulders and look down while they chat don't have enough confidence. That probably happens because they are shy or lack self-esteem. With a vigorous stance and pushing the chest out they can show their utmost confidence.

To be able to comprehend a discussion thoroughly, someone must acknowledge the secrets of body language. Once this is understood properly, it's not complicated to discern what the entire discussion is about.

CHAPTER TWELVE

INTERPRETING BODY LANGUAGE

To explain body language, one must examine the gestures, facial expressions and actions connected to another person's behavior. Interpreting the body language can be done based on the individual culture and situation and represents a key aspect of communication.

In our daily interactions, we should be able to recognize the messages that are sent to us during a conversation. Language interpretation must be done with subtlety, so that people that are analyzed will not figure this out. If we don't consider this aspect, this will lead the other person to feel awkward and annoyed.

In this article you can find many tips on how to examine and interpret someone's body language.

Eyes – When you see that someone has dilated pupils, this is a sign of interest in your discussion. If they don't maintain eye contact with you and their eyes look at other things in the room, it probably shows that they aren't interested in the discussion. Looking to the side could indicate a sense of guilt, while looking down shows they feel ashamed.

Eyebrows – When someone raises his eyebrows it usually indicates shock or surprise. Flicking the eyebrows while looking at someone else means that the person understands you or greets you.

Hands and arms – One key factor in interpreting body language is hands interpretation. When someone has his palms opened, this shows his state of calmness and comfort. All the same, arm folding is a sign that the person is disapproving, angry and troubled. When the arms are in open positions, the person illustrates a sense of sincerity and that he agrees with what the other person says.

Feet – The position of the feet is likewise a great feature when we examine someone's body language. If the person's feet are pointing at you when you are standing opposite to him, this is a sign that the person is happy in your presence. Their eyes will gaze at you and their head will point in your direction. If his feet are not directed towards you, it's possible that their head and eyes will point in another direction, too. This could show that there is less interest in the conversation or a sense of annoyance.

Legs – When someone is sitting down or standing with legs shoulder width apart, it means that he is calm. If the person has his legs crossed while standing, it might show that the person is shy. If, on the other hand, he is seated with his legs crossed, this means that the person is introverted and conservative.

These are the basic features that you can utilize to examine a person's body language. If you want to master the interpretation of body language, you must exercise these tools frequently. The more you work on them, the more you will increase your skills and achieve subtlety in your conversations.

CHAPTER THIRTEEN

USING BODY LANGUAGE TO UNCOVER LIES

Examining body language can be useful, primarily if someone is lying to you. If a person pays close attention to the body language of someone else, he can immediately see if that person is not telling the truth.

Most of the times, people cannot pick up on someone who is lying. This shouldn't be the case because it is actually very easy to find out. When someone is smiling, you can immediately tell what state he is in. There are people who smile just to make an impression and those that show a real smile. Those that smile just to make an impression use only the muscles around the mouth, while those that laugh from all their heart use more muscles and the cheeks. If someone dodges eye contact, it means he is trying to hide something. The reason is that he knows that people can read this in his eyes. It's not so easy to lie and maintain a sincere face at the same time. Usually, when someone is lying, his eyes are wondering in every direction continuously. If you have such a person in front of you, he is only telling lies to you, because that is the actual body language of a liar.

A person that is lying defends himself constantly. This type of situation can be encountered quite often. Someone can change his tone or scream at you when lying. Detecting this type of body language is necessary in order to find out if someone is telling lies to you. A person who is not telling the truth will do fake gestures regularly. For example, he will pretend he is shocked. Another behavior you may notice is a delay in their reaction. The tone of his voice is also worth taking into consideration. For example, if someone speaks about love to another person and doesn't sound too convincing, he is probably lying and you can immediately see from his voice that he is not sincere. Some folks are tense when they lie, and they try to hide their faces using hand gestures like scratching their noses or speaking with one hand on their mouths. There are numerous people that lie when flirting because they want to make themselves more appealing. You can tell this by observing the rapid swift in their body language. If you are attentive to these swifts, you will not have any problems to determine when someone is not telling the truth. Examining hand movements are also useful, because people who lie frequently play with their hair or twitch their fingers. You will encounter this type of body language quite often.

Body language modifies when a person is trying to lie. That is why you must have the skills to detect when someone doesn't tell the truth to you.

CHAPTER FOURTEEN

COMPREHENDING BODY LANGUAGE SIGNALS

A key factor of every conversation is body language. By comprehending body language and gestures you will manage any situation the right way. That is why it is extremely important.

Eye contact is one of the key most important body language signals. When someone emanates confidence he makes constant eye contact with the audience. The tone of a person's voice indicates the degree of confidence. If someone doesn't make eye contact frequently, this shows that he is probably shy, anxious, or doesn't have self-esteem. People that look down often or at their annotations are considered shy or nervous. They usually speak with a low voice. When a speaker is in front of an audience his body language, gestures and eye contact must show confidence. People in the audience provide the speaker with info about their state of mind. The ones that show interest will maintain eye contact with the speaker continuously and will focus on what he talks about. People that don't care about the discussion will have less eye contact with the speaker or no eye contact at all. There will also be some people with raised eyebrows; this is a sign that they disagree with what is being discussed. These types of body language signals are worth considering because they show critical info to the speaker.

There are also body language signals that can be read through facial expressions. Facial expressions represent an effortless way of reading people. Anxious people illustrate their nervousnesses by continually looking down. Usually, when they smile, you can sense that they don't have full confidence. People that are fearful or wondering about something will look distracted. Examining their body language signals will enable you to discover more about these people. A person's stance will provide you with more info about him. If a person is in a bend position often, it means that he is not confident and shy. In opposition, a strong stance shows confidence. People that are confident tend to smile more. If they show a natural, warm smile, we can definitely say they have confidence. Examining someone's hand can also provide us with more body language information. If a person's hands are in motion often it's an indication that the he is interested in the conversation, but if he is continually twitching his fingers it means he is anxious and not interested.

In order to fully comprehend body language signals, you must have the skills to gather as much info as you can. People who control this will always be one step above others in any discussion.

CHAPTER FIFTEEN

MAKING EYE CONTACT THROUGH BODY LANGUAGE

Eyes are extremely important in a conversation because they show a person's state quickly. Actually, they are the most essential part of the human body that can be used in a non-verbal communication. There are numerous connotations to the appearance of the eyes and how the muscles work around the eyes. If the person is glazing somewhere, it will also have a certain connotation. The reason for this is that examining eye contact and body language is as important as reading any other body language feature.

Let's not forget how people interact when they are in the middle of a regular discussion. If someone is looking you straight in the eye, it is probably because he wants to prevail on you in a battle or he may be focused on the subject that is discussed. If the other person is looking at the ground, then it is a sign of resignation. The speaker that is looking down cannot prevail on the other person and this means that he will withdraw and not argue with what the speaker says.

Many studies have been done to comprehend body language and eye contact. One of them states that every time someone wants to recall something, he is looking to the left. If someone is looking to the right, it indicates he is thinking about creating something or he invents a lie. These details will give us useful info about the person we discuss with. That being said, we should not forget that a few of these signs will be different from person to person. For some folks these signs of looking left or right could be changed.

Let's suppose that you are male and discover that a person is attractive, what would you do in this case? You would gaze at her face for a moment and then shift your eyes from top to bottom, right? This is also true for women too. Thus, when we talk about body language and eye contact, we should also notice where the speaker's eyes are looking because it will show us what his mindset is focused on. For example, if a woman is attracted by a man, she is most likely looking at his chest and neck. Likewise, a man will make regular eye contact with a woman's face, neck area, and hands if he finds her appealing.

There are numerous sources on the Internet where you can find information about body language and eye contact. Practice what you have learned here as often as possible so that the next time you have a conversation with someone you can determine his thoughts based on his gestures. It's not hard to obtain results, but you must master the art of reading human behavior.

CHAPTER SIXTEEN

EXAMPLES OF BODY LANGUAGE

Many single folks have the intention of meeting their soul mate. Therefore, they go to bars and other places with their friends, hoping that the person they are meant to be with will show up. You probably heard about the saying 'actions speak louder than words'. In this case, actions are actually body language, gestures that one could make when talking to another person. Although there are young people that don't understand the other person's body language signals right, if they study this subject more it will benefit them in the future.

Women observe body language gestures, more careful than men do. They also believe in the zodiac and think that a man's sense of humor and character is closely related to the body language he illustrates. There are many women that learn about these matters because they believe it will help them choose the best partner.

This also holds true for a few men who evaluate women for these body language examples. A woman that flicks her hair while she is looking at you is one body language example that shows that she has remarked your presence and is interested in you.

The first meeting is very important because both parties will form their first impression about each other. Many people nowadays, try to find out body language examples so that they can gauge someone. For example, you might express something that is the exact opposite of what you actually feel inside. Remember the saying your 'actions speak louder than words'.

The simplest methods for practicing appropriate body language example will assist you in your search for the woman of your dreams. On the other hand, people who deliver the wrong messages through their gestures will not have a long lasting conversation with the woman they seek.

Most men grumble about how tough it is to be accepted by a woman, primarily because they talk about one thing when they actually refer to another. This can be really hard if you are married to a wife that says 'yes' when she means 'no'. Did you evaluate her body language examples correctly? You have to pay attention to this.

Most women oftentimes illustrate body language examples that look almost the same. At the end of this chapter you will find a few body language examples that depict a woman's brain.

When a woman doesn't feel safe, she is always fixing her hair. If a woman is anxious she usually bites her nails. A sign of a woman's eagerness is finger drumming, while frustration can be shown by hand clasping. If you remember these basic body language examples you will have no problem in finding the girl of your dreams. Comprehending these body language examples with diligence will ensure that you exceed your friends in this regard.

CHAPTER SEVENTEEN

COMPREHENDING BODY LANGUAGE CLUES

Body language is a form of nonverbal connection that uses body gestures, postures and eye contact. In general, people illustrate and comprehend these body language cues without being aware of them. A study conducted by Albert Mehrabian shows that 93% of all the human communication relies on body language cues and only 7% of human communication is revealed through actual words. Although these numbers are contested by some people, other researchers believe that at least 60-70% of all communication consists of body language cues.

Actually, body language cues show the attitude and the emotional state of mind of an individual. For example, aggression, attentiveness, pleasure and boredom are emotions that can be illustrated by body language cues of a person. Kinesics is the discipline that studies body language cues and expressions and it is used in fields such as law enforcement or military when different people are interrogated. People that are qualified in kinesics can read body language cues and find out if someone is telling the truth or not.

There are multiple body language cues that have multiple connotations. For instance, when someone crosses his arms to the chest it means that the person is unknowingly building an invisible barrier between himself and people around him. This is probably one of the strongest and most fundamental body language cues expressed by people. If the majority of people that accompany a person are friendly, this posture will portray that this person is examined thoroughly about the discussed items. That being said, if the situation is combative, then this is a sign of adversity.

Eye movement is likewise a very powerful type of body language. Constant eye contact shows that a person has positive thoughts about the speaker. Nonetheless, it could also illustrate that the person doesn't have enough confidence in the speaker to move his eyes off him. When a person doesn't maintain eye contact with the other it's a sign that he might be lying or that he has a negative state of mind. However, there are some people that suffer from anxiety disorders that fail to keep eye contact without feeling annoyed. There are also a few other body language cues that have certain implications. For example, eagerness can be detected when someone has both hands on the hips, while one hand rubbing the other hand is a sign that the person is comforting himself.

Body language cues are an essential element of human communication, and people transmit tons of information unknowingly through these cues. It is very important to acknowledge that the info is transmitted primarily through a person's body language cues and, secondly, through actual language.

CHAPTER EIGHTEEN

ALLUREMENT THROUGH BODY LANGUAGE

When accompanied by people of the opposite sex, both males and females have a transition in their body languages. Men will maintain a firm stance and will not illustrate a loused posture in front of women. He will try to express confidence and try to look more dominant by expanding his chest out and detracting his stomach.

A charming body language is confined to a certain degree and gestures correlated to that of women. If a man finds a woman appealing, he will focus on his masculine gestures to show his manhood. Some examples of such gestures are styling his hair, wearing enticing clothes and also lunging his chin forward. Another interesting gesture a man often does to express his manhood is tucking his thumbs into his belt.

A woman will display allurement gestures through hints and symbols that a man can see, so that he will understand her feelings. Most of the times women associate different types of signals knowingly and unknowingly when they express their feelings. This behavior oftentimes seems insincere to a man and may distract him and make him try to fend off the woman.

Hair flicking is the most frequently allurement gesture used by women and is holds true especially for women with short hair. When someone sees a person that looks appealing, the only thing that restrains him from talking to that person is the lack of confidence. When someone is lacking confidence you could see him touching things or leaning against something by using his body because that is the way body language is portrayed. To convey an alluring body language you must walk with grace, maintain a firm stance and don't make fast movements. You should also avoid looking down.

Remember that your delicate attitude towards the other person creates allurement. When you are sitting you must not be stiff and you should keep your legs and arms together. Men tend to spread their limbs on many occasions, even if they occupy another person's space. Nevertheless, you should do this in a natural way, and not make it seem like it's done in a private way. Be relaxed and talk with confidence. People that accompany you will feel more calm and confident if you express these things through your body language.

CHAPTER NINETTEN

UTILIZING BODY LANGUAGE IN YOUR FAVOUR

Comprehending the significance of human body language will be a huge advantage for you. There are choices you probably wouldn't have made if you had known the secrets of body language earlier.

When a couple is near a break-up or divorce the most common reasons are unfaithfulness and treason. Oftentimes these problems have surfaced right from the beginning, but people fail to understand the body language of the other partner. People can try to put on many masks, but their body always tells the truth. Thus, a person's true intent is revealed by the body in many circumstances and you can utilize this info to understand people better.

You will avoid being unhappy or pessimistic if you can interpret the handwriting of your spouse properly. You must have the will to act on problems before they lead to a divorce or break-up. For instance, if you know that you cannot avoid divorce or break-up, you can at least restrain its consequences by preparing yourself before it happens. If you act like this it's quite possible that your spouse will not suspect that you understood her body language and you knew what will happen ahead of time, so she might argue with you.

After a person goes through a rough period in his life he usually says 'had I known that, I would have done things differently'. Understanding body language and mastering the significance of gestures will remove this saying from your mind and will allow you to foresee things before they happen and ensure that you only make good choices in your life.

Let's suppose for a moment that you interpret an appealing person's body language and you find out e or she is not a reliable and sincere person; you have to judge for yourself if you really want to begin a romantic relationship with such a person. If you choose to go in a relationship having the thought of changing the other person, you are fooling yourself and you are responsible for that.

If you can interpret human body gestures the right way, you won't be in trouble. The information laid out in this book will change your relationship dramatically and will keep you away from pitfalls. A pitfall means nothing if you cannot acknowledge it or if you continue to act based on emotions and desires.

For in vain is the net spread in the sight of any bird...

(Proverbs 1:17)

A woman who finds out her partner is aggressive, threatening or even capable of rape should stay away from him if she hasn't lost the sense of reality. This is another situation that can be avoided by interpreting body language.

If someone is talking to you while at the same time looking in another direction, you will immediately figure out that he might lie to you, and you can make the right choices that will protect your future and your relation.

Don't forget that if you have the appropriate info, it will encourage you to act the right way and when you don't have the proper info you will not act right. So practicing body language interpretation will have a deep impact on your relationship and entire life.

However, if a person's body language illustrates a charming, loving and helpful character and you seem appealing to him, you should judge wisely if you respond with the same type of body language and agree to go on a date with that person.

Many conflicts and disputes can be avoided by practicing the art of interpreting body language. This information can ensure that you will pass through major issues that might affect you otherwise in your daily life. Your partner may wonder if you are a fortune teller that knows all kinds of things ahead of time. Communication is the best way to maintain a relationship and furthermore build sufficient trust between partners.

Someone that has a relationship with an introverted partner will consider these things very precious because they will know how to read the body gestures of such a person. Even though an introvert doesn't communicate too well, his body will show his true feelings. There are a few relationships that have ended because of the introverts' unwillingness to communicate. The ability to discover, master and figure out how to read the body signs of an introvert will assist you in communicating the right way and solving matters with your partner. The human body sends out a message through nonverbal communication that can be unraveled and this message is directed at the true state of an introverts' heart without pressuring him.

Create a profound relationship by changing the way you understand body language gesture,s and by mastering its principles.

These principles will provide you the means to manage your relationship correctly, protect your heart, find adequate solutions and will give you time to contemplate on things that you know will occur. In case you fail to put your relationship on the right track, you will not have a depression as a result and you will not be taken by surprise. Your mind will be at ease with the situation because you had some time to cope with it. Even though it might still hurt, it won't be as painful as a sudden break of faith.

Many people say "Yes, we divorced because we had irreconcilable differences", but this should not be applied to a person who understands how to interpret body language properly. Such a person will have a new comprehension about his life because he has seen the discrepancies beforehand and he can make a decision about entering a relationship or a marriage. He will not be tended to marry or be with someone if he is aware of the risk ahead of time.

A Nigerian star confessed about his marriage: "Our problems started immediately after the wedding, but we decided to continue our relationship thinking that we will sort things out. However, we didn't manage to sort things out and we separated. We split up a while ago, but we didn't want to make it known to everyone. I am positive the Lord has his ways of doing things." This statement indicates that this couple understood the outcome of their relationship from body language, but still engaged in it waiting for things to happen. In reality, you cannot go into a relationship thinking you will change the other person, the only person whom you can change is yourself. Only by making changes to yourself can you expect to modify your partner's behavior.

Someone who had affairs before marriage will also have this tendency after he gets married too. Therefore, if you later blame your partner for extra-marital issues and request separation, you should be prepared and take responsibility for this compromise.

In the Huffington Post, David Wygant answered someone's question about men who end their marriages suddenly: "Why do men in their 20's start dating women while being just married? My partner woke up one day and told me he wants to move on. A few weeks later he met another woman and married her while we were still living with the kids in the basement of his parents' home. How could this be happening? Shouldn't this woman be concerned with his situation? A long time has passed since then and I feel I cannot ever trust another man again. I just want to understand why these things happen, that's all...

"Here is your answer:

A man doesn't just leave for no reason. Many men and women don't communicate properly. A marriage that lasts 20 years probably had warning signs for at least ten years.

A marriage cannot end overnight. You can't say that after 20 years of marriage someone wakes up one day and tells his partner 'Hey, we should consider a divorce. Last night was awesome, but I want to split up with you."

If a marriage suddenly ends, it means the ending process started long ago, but one partner failed to see the warning signs.

If you had a hard time coping with your divorce and analyzing why the marriage ended, you really need to think about the things I just mentioned.

One of the most important things you must do is to recall if you ever felt that things are not going the right way, because there were warning signs about this for sure.

Think about how often he was away from home or if he worked after hours.

Think about how often you communicated with him or how often you were intimate with him. There are a lot of things that probably were not on track in your marriage. A marriage doesn't just end; it ends slowly, after a certain period of time.

Try to recall the discussions about your relationship. How often did you argue with him? Did you talk about the future of your marriage?

There are many people, both men and women that avoid going into the profound issues of what I call the intimacy zone.

They incline to leave things as they are and they fear to say what they truly feel in their heart. And then what follows is usually separation or sudden end of their marriage.

Here comes the part that many people cannot figure out: how to deal with it. You shouldn't take these things personally just because you were blind in your first encounters with that person. Most likely, you chose to be blind, knowing in your heart that you are not truly satisfied with your partner.

If you search deeper you will probably find out there are many things you weren't satisfied about. A lot of times, women focus on the pain they feel in their heart and won't think about the real motives for which they entered that relationship.

You won't resolve anything if you just complain that your relationship didn't work out and didn't satisfy you.

You should probably focus your attention inward; it's time to dig deeper to find the exact motives why your marriage fell apart.

Things don't manifest only on the surface. You must have the courage to face reality and move on in your life. Just keep in mind that you should not repeat the same mistakes with another man in the future.

Don't become introverted by locking up your feelings and avoiding communication. And always avoid being drowsy.

Life is a continuous lesson and we must go through hardships and getting past them will make you stronger. You should consider the multitude of men out there that want to meet the girl of their dreams."

- http://www.huffingtonpost.com/david-wygant/the-number-1-reason-marri_b_3047498.html

At this point we must admit that even when the handwriting is so clear, there are some people that continue to make the wrong choices because they give credit to their uncontrolled feelings rather than a logical judgment. Only when their emotions will become weaker and conflicts emerge will they understand that judgment is far more important than feelings. You should be clear about the fact that the interpretation of body language, gestures and analyzing things has clearly been two separate factors that influence the final decision you make.

You can utilize the information provided by body language interpretation to change your whole relationship and life. If your judgment provides evidence that you should not be involved with someone, you should handle your emotions well and don't let them influence you too much when making an important decision.

Most likely, you aren't reading this book by chance. You will benefit from this book more than you imagine because you will figure out how to maintain a long lasting relationship or how to meet the right person. I hope you will be able to achieve your relationship goals by practicing and utilizing body language interpretation.

MB Relationship Coaching & Consultancy can help you deal with relationship issues or challenges through in-depth and life changing coaching. We have helped numerous people, both singles and married to focus positively and take their current relationships from the current state to the expected state.

Visit:

www.marcusbenson.eu

www.unbreakablerelationships.com

ABOUT THE AUTHOR

Dr. Marcus S. Benson is the president of Relationship Coaching & Consultancy, Inc., Ireland. He is a sought after motivational speaker, author, conference speaker and a certified relationship coach, empowering relationships with ease. One of his popular quotes is "Relationship is to be enjoyed and not to be endured". For over twenty years he has used his knowledge, experience and skills to turn relationships around, thereby bringing about blissfulness and total fulfillment. He has a master's degree in counselling psychology. His practical and compassionate approach makes him stand out amongst many. Dr. Marcus S. Benson , who is a graduate of the National University of Ireland, Northwestern Christian University, Life College, USA, Blackford Centre for life coaching, UK and Mental Health Academy, Australia coaches with great confidence. He is highly positive, proactive, results driven in his professional approach to getting his clients discover themselves and find practical ways to resolve their issues and achieve outstanding results.

MB Relationship Coaching & Consultancy, Ireland.

Empowering Your Relationship With Ease.

www.marcusbenson.eu

Managing Love, Passion and Romance

- Unbreakable Relationships Clinic

- Unbreakable Relationships Media

Tel: +353(0)870912166

www.unbreakablerelationships.blogspot.com